BUYING
A HOUSE IN
FRANCE

BUYING A HOUSE IN FRANCE

DAVID SIZER

Macdonald
Queen Anne Press

A QUEEN ANNE PRESS BOOK

© David Sizer 1991

First published in Great Britain in 1991 by
Queen Anne Press, a division of
Macdonald & Co (Publishers) Ltd
Orbit House
1 New Fetter Lane
London EC4A 1AR

A member of Maxwell Macmillan Pergamon Publishing Corporation

Maps drawn by Hardlines
Cover photograph by Landscapes Only

Please note that while every effort has been made to ensure that all the facts, comments, laws and their interpretations included in this book are accurate and up-to-date, neither the author nor the publishers are able to accept any responsibility for the accuracy or contents of this book, nor for any consequential loss that may be incurred for whatever reason.

A CIP catalogue record for this book is available from the British Library

ISBN 0–356–19752–2

Typeset by Selectmove Limited, London
Printed and bound in Great Britain by Mackays of Chatham plc

CONTENTS

DEDICATION

To Caroline Walker in gratitude for her unstinting help with the purchase of my own house and for her guidance on the *compromis* and the *acte de vente*.

Caroline is the only person I know who is able to begin a sentence in immaculate English and complete it in flawless French. Without a pause and with a perfect accent throughout.

Which is why I am so certain that the letters in the appendices are indeed in impeccable French.

Thank you Caroline.

INTRODUCTION

Finding and buying a house can be a time-consuming and irritating activity that we endure because we have the hope that sometime, somehow, somewhere we will find the dream house that makes it all worthwhile.

And if house-hunting is like that in the United Kingdom, it can be far worse if your dream house is to be located across the Channel in France. For in the UK it is perfectly possible to view a house for no greater expenditure than a Sunday afternoon drive and £5 for the petrol. But, if your house is located in, say, Cognac, the figures are more likely to be three days and £200.

This does not mean that your dream house in France is impossible, but it does mean that if costs are to be controlled, wasted visits must be kept to a minimum. And that means not looking at houses before you have decided on the district and whether you wish to live in a city, town, village, or hamlet.

Once you have found the house it gets a little better. House prices in France are about half UK prices (at the time of writing), the legal system is more rational – one lawyer can represent both parties – mortgage rates are a dizzy 10½ percent, and building costs are about the same as in the UK. Of course this does not mean there will be no snags. There are incompetent lawyers in France, just as there are in the UK. And estate agents. And plumbers. Moreover, interest rates can go up as well as down, even in France, and woodworm and dry rot know no boundaries.

The material in this book is based on the experiences of people who have bought houses in France. It is offered not only in the hope that you will draw a modicum of comfort from the knowledge that others have suffered before you, but also that you will, perhaps, be able to avoid the problems they have encountered.

PART ONE

FINDING IT

INTRODUCTION

The reasons for deciding to buy a house in France range from the cuisine, to a typically English summer via 36 hours at Alicante airport, but, whatever the reason, all eventually lead to the question: where?

This is not an easy question to answer as France is more than twice the size of the UK. Of course holiday trips have given many of us an idea of some parts of the country, but fond memories of a happy fortnight five years ago are not necessarily the best basis for choosing where to live. Nor is it a good idea to base your search on a weekly browse through the property pages of the Sunday newspapers with a view to approaching the estate agents and individuals who advertise there. A single house, or a handful of houses, is hardly going to be representative of the range of property available in a French *département* the size of Yorkshire, for there will be just as great a variety of scenery and industry there as in Yorkshire. Consider the difference between Bradford and Harrogate and remember that, however attractive the property may sound, you know little of its location and could spend precious time and money on a wasted trip.

In any case, why allow 'where' to be determined by what happens to be advertised in the UK press? Surely it is much better to decide upon the area and then search for the house? When house-hunting in the UK, the 'where' is

FINDING IT!

mostly determined by the need to live relatively close to work or to a good school, but these constraints do not apply in France unless one is emigrating. France, for most of us, offers the opportunity to buy a house for fun, for sheer pleasure, a place for our holidays, for our children's holidays, for our retirement. So why rush at it? Why not take your time and make sure that when you buy, you buy what you want, where you want it?

And if the range of property offered in the UK press may be incomplete, what of the house prices being asked? They may seem good value when measured against UK prices, but how do they compare with the going rate in France?

If you were a French estate agent working with an English agent with whom you had to split the commission if he provided the buyer, would you not try and sell in France first and pocket all the commission? Only later, when it had become obvious that the charms and value of a particular property had escaped your countrymen, would you pass the details to the English agent. After all, better half than nothing. This is not to say there may not be houses advertised in the UK press that represent excellent value for money. But until you have done your homework you will not know which is which. *Caveat emptor* reigns.

Nor is it a sound tactic to rely on a UK agent's description of a house, firstly because the probability that the agent has seen the property is extremely low (the French agent who supplied him or her with the information may not have seen it either), and secondly there is the special way that estate agents have with words, a skill that can be used to describe a house as having a 'semi-rural aspect' when it has a pig farm on one side and a

steel works on the other, or as having 'river frontage' when the 'river' (a stagnant, overgrown brook) is half a mile away and lies across (somebody else's) hostile terrain.

Moreover, the probability that the UK agent knows the district is not much better than his knowledge of the house, for his position, more often than not, is akin to that of a travel agent eulogizing about a hotel he has never visited in a resort he has never seen. For example, at a recent French property exhibition I visited, a sales person, realizing that I knew the area, fixed me with a confidential smile and asked, 'Are there any foreigners there?' The answer, of course, was yes, I'm afraid so. They are called French.

In circumstances such as these it is easy to visit France to view a house only to find that the house and district are not what you thought they were, and that your trip has been a complete waste of time and money. Naturally an estate agent cannot be held responsible for the errors or omissions that led to your wasted trip, oh dear me, no!

It is always best to begin with some prudent groundwork. There is no reason why this should not include a weekly trawl through the property pages of the Sunday glossies, requesting further information about advertised properties, having your name put on various lists, or even, if you must, visiting property exhibitions. But do not, at this stage, agree to view in France, and at all times – but particularly at overseas property exhibitions – remember this rule: the probability of a rip-off is directly proportional to the width of the pin stripe and the depth of the cleavage.

CHAPTER ONE

CHOOSING THE QUARTER

In my view, the question 'Where?' is best answered in stages. The first stage is to cut France into quarters and choose the quarter you prefer. There is no divine law that says you must divide by four; Caesar, you will remember, divided by three. In fact, any number other than one is good because posing alternatives imposes discipline. You could, for example, try dividing the country in half. Do you prefer the bottom half to the top half? The eastern half to the western?

In making your choice, it is sensible to keep a number of points in mind:

CLIMATE

France is big, with a climate in the north-west – in Brittany – similar to that of Cornwall, and in the south-east – in Provence – not too far from that of the Sahara, at least in the summer. Obviously, then, climate is an important factor in your choice. August temperatures on the Mediterranean coast can be over 33°C (90°F), on the Atlantic coast over 27°C (80°F) and on the Channel coast around a more recognizable 21°C (70°F). In winter many parts of France are colder than the UK, and the general rule is that the further you are from the coast the colder it is likely to be. In the extreme west of Brittany, sticking out into the Atlantic and lapped by the final vestige of the Gulf Stream, they panic if there is snow, while in the Alps they panic if there is none. It is also worth noting that the further south and west you go the longer the summer is likely to be and the shorter the winter.

SCENERY

What sort of scenery makes you feel comfortable? Do you prefer flat land and big skies? Or dramatic cliffs, gorges and snow-clad peaks? Or something softer with chestnuts, willows and meadows?

WHAT WILL YOU DO THERE?

If you enjoy the beach or messing about in boats, then you will need to be within 50 kilometres (30 miles) of one of the coasts. If climbing or skiing are your hobbies, then the Alps or the Pyrenees are going to be attractive. If you prefer rivers and fishing, or woods and walking, then France is your oyster for it abounds with rivers and forests. What you are going to do need not be limited to the physical. All of France enjoys considerable cultural activity, and relevant information on the performing arts and on exhibitions and museums is easily obtained from the French Tourist Office (Appendix E, page 85)

HOW OFTEN WILL YOU VISIT?

Unless you are very rich and able to afford a weekly flight from Heathrow to Bordeaux, a cottage close to that city is not really a practical proposition for a weekend retreat. If it is a weekend cottage that you want, then something about an hour's drive from one of the Channel ports would be ideal. If, however, your house is going to be used for holidays, then nearly all of France lies within a day's drive from the Channel ports. The *autoroute* network is important (Appendix B, page 80).

HOW TO GET THERE

The highway is not the only method of travel that is available. The French *autoroute* network is substantial, but there are considerable gaps in the network in some areas. SNCF (*Société Nationale des Chemins de Fer Français*) has a more comprehensive network. If you are planning to use your house for retirement you may not relish the prospect of a long drive, preferring rail as a sensible alternative. Moreover, the new TGV (*Train à Grande Vitesse*) service is expanding steadily and journey times are falling. Paris to Nantes, for example, is now down to two hours. A map of the main SNCF network can be found in Appendix

C (page 82), and the TGV routes in Appendix D (page 84). Flying is also a possibility, and there are airports at Nantes, Bordeaux, Toulouse, Strasbourg, Montpellier, Marseille, Lille, Biarritz, Nice and Lyon. For many of the above, services are reduced in winter, and there are none to Biarritz.

SUMMARY

When choosing the quarter do not forget:

- Climate
- Scenery
- What will you do there?
- How often will you visit?
- How to get there

Such a list may seem daunting, and infer a massive expenditure of time, energy, and money in the search of – what? Just a quarter? In fact, much of your homework can be done as a desk exercise. To begin with, you probably have memories and photographs of holidays past. How do they measure against the criteria listed above? Then there is the French Tourist Office, ever ready to help potential tourists by supplying information on the scenery, climate, and available activities of just about every *département* of France. Nor should you forget your local reference library, which can be encouraged and/or cajoled into supplying you with information, be it historical, political, or industrial. Instead of spending the winter months flicking through package-holiday brochures, you could be flicking through the information you need to select your quarter, and to identify the districts that are of interest to you.

Whatever you do, do *not* begin to make trips to look at houses before you have decided on the quarter. Remember, each wasted trip adds £200 to the cost of your house. Instead, just keep trawling through the newspapers, plundering the estate agents for more information, and, if you must, visiting property exhibitions. But whatever you do, do not forget the previous warning about salespeople.

CHAPTER TWO

FINDING THE DISTRICT

Having selected the quarter you are interested in, it is time to zoom in and narrow the focus. Again, there are a number of points you will need to keep in mind, all of them aspects of the well-known adage, 'The three most important factors to consider when selecting a house are *position*, *position* and *position*.'

ON THE COAST OR INLAND?

This is of concern to those who seek beaches and sailing. Do you wish to be on the coast or a little further inland? The drawback with the French coast is that summer is a mad-house, particularly August, and the rest of the year it is dead, closed and shuttered. A short distance inland, however, the summer season often hardly exists because the locals farm or grow grapes and ignore the holiday season.

Generally, you will find prices are higher on the coast than inland. There may also be more security available inland, because a 'living' village in winter is more likely to keep a benevolent eye on your empty house than a deserted resort. Of course a house in a resort will allow you to walk rather than drive to the beach with its attendant parking problems, especially in August. The further north you choose to go the shorter the summer season will be, and the further south the longer it will be. But wherever you go, there *will* be a summer season. After all, people are not on holiday for the entire year.

What has been said here in respect to the coastal fringe applies equally to other tourist centres in summer, and to ski resorts in winter.

CITY, TOWN, VILLAGE OR HAMLET?

The next point to consider is what size place do you wish to live in? A city with multiple traffic lights, one-way streets, and a morning rush-hour? Or a town with only one set of lights but with several hairdressers, restaurants and a supermarket? Or perhaps a village with no traffic lights, a *pâtisserie*, two restaurants, a butcher and a village shop? Why not a hamlet with no shops, where the baker, butcher and perhaps fishmonger arrive at set times each day or week?

As a general guide, a city or a town is almost certain to have an SNCF station; a village perhaps, but doubtful; a hamlet almost certainly not.

Most places will have electricity, although some very remote farmhouses may still be without, and the same applies to piped water. Sewage disposal in hamlets and villages will be of the individual septic tank variety, with generally only towns and cities having sewage systems and piped town gas. Elsewhere gas comes in bottles from local distributors or from supermarkets.

SUMMARY

- On the coast or inland?
- City, town, village or hamlet?

CHAPTER THREE

MAKING CONTACT

You should by now have narrowed your area of search to a particular *département* or group of *départements*, and possibly to specific districts and towns/villages within that area. It is now time to start thinking about your house, and how you are going to discover it. Once again, there are things to do and thoughts to bear in mind.

MAPS

You will need a map, or rather maps, as a scale of at least 1:25000 is necessary. The 'Serie Bleue' by the *Institut Geographie National* is good, and an essential tool to weed out those desirable residences that nestle 'neath *autoroute* bridges, back on to TGV high-speed railway lines, or cringe terrified at the end of military runways. The maps are not cheap, but they are an invaluable tool for avoiding unnecessary and wasted trips.

SYNDICAT D'INITIATIVE

You will need to get in touch with the people who have houses to sell. In France, as in the UK, there are estate agents in the house-selling market, although in France estate agents account for only around 25 percent of the market. The remainder is shared by the local solicitor (*notaire*), and individuals, who have the largest slice. You will need to get in touch with all three. The place to start is with the *Office de Tourisme* of the *département*(s) in which you are interested. Addresses are available from the French Government Tourist Office (Appendix E, page 85).

The *département Office de Tourisme* will be able to provide a wide range of information including the addresses of the local *Syndicat d'Initiative* offices, which you will find in the larger towns in your selected area. To help you, I have included a letter written in impeccable – well, *I* think it is impeccable – French (Appendix F, page 86).

Syndicats d'Initiative originally were established to promote tourism but seem willing to do almost anything to encourage interest in their district. What is needed is a nice letter saying how much you like their area, how you would like to buy a house there, and how grateful you would be if they could let you have the names and addresses of local estate agents, *notaires* who sell houses, and the names and addresses of local newspapers that, of course, carry advertisements from the individuals selling direct as well as from estate agents. To help you I have included a letter written in French that asks for exactly those things (Appendix G, page 87).

BANK ACCOUNTS

It is sensible to establish a French bank account because it makes life a lot simpler to have a local source of money. Moreover, francs bought at the commercial rate offer a better exchange rate than francs 'bought' when you use Access, Visa, or Eurocheque. Finally, having a bank account is a necessary preparation for the day when you will need to move money to France for the house.

The best course of action is to approach your UK bank and ask them which French bank they correspond with. You can then establish whether this bank has a branch in the largest town in your chosen area. It is a simple matter to buy francs through your UK bank and have them sent to this branch to be held for you. Another sensible move is to ask your UK bank to send a letter of introduction confirming what a jolly good sort you are, pillar of society, most certainly not the type to undermine the Republic, or write cheques that bounce, etc., etc. After all, if my bank did it for me I do not see why your bank should not do it for you.

Allow a couple of weeks for all of the above to happen, the money may well have to travel to the French bank via your UK bank's head office and the French bank's head office. On your next visit to France you will need to call at the bank, introduce yourself, show them your passport to prove you are who you say you are, show them something official that confirms you live at the address you have given, for example, a poll-tax demand or an electricity bill – but *not* a final demand or a summons as that might make them worry unduly about the reliability of the letter of introduction!

You will have to go through the tedious routine of specimen signatures and then wait perhaps a week or two for your cheque-book to arrive. Once you have been through the process you will realize what a good idea it was to get it done early and not wait until you are sweating about getting your house.

THE HOUSE

By now you will have received replies from the *Syndicat d'Initiative* and will be ready to write to the *notaires*, *agents immobiliers*, and the newspapers whose addresses you requested. First, however, you will need to finalize your thoughts on the sort of house or *appartement* you want to buy.

It looks silly to write this, and it probably seems silly to read it, but houses in France are either old or new. That is to say, in my experience it seems that houses are either more than one hundred years old, or less than twenty. Much the same can be said for *appartements*. Put another way, do you wish to have a traditional, perhaps stone-built, property, or a modern, newly built property? Do you want an old property that has been restored, or would you prefer to restore it yourself? Do you want a garage? A large garden or a small garden?

You will also need to draw on the knowledge you have accumulated from your weekly trawls through the overseas property pages as you will need to give an indication of the price you wish to pay. The prices you will have seen quoted in the UK probably will not have understated the market price in France. There is also the need to counter the tendency of estate agents to send particulars of properties priced at or above the price you quote, but never below, so I recommend taking 25 percent off the listed prices when indicating what you expect to spend. If you fail to find anything of interest at that price you can always go up, but it is difficult to go down as prices, once fixed in an estate agent's mind, seem immune to the law of gravity. In other words, act on house prices in France in much the same way you would in the UK.

The difference of course is that you will need to communicate your requirements in French. To help you I have supplied (again in impeccable French) letters to *agents immobiliers* and *notaires* (Appendix H, page 88), which include gaps for you to enter the appropriate number of rooms, and so on. There is also a letter to the local newspaper (Appendix J, page 93) asking if they could supply you on a subscription basis. I am talking here about the local 'freebie' newspaper which, because most houses in France are sold by individuals, should contain a good selection of properties. Of course you will also need to understand the replies you receive, and what is being said about the properties offered to you. You will find a glossary of relevant terms in Appendix I (page 90), but also, because you will need it sooner or later, get yourself a good French-English, English-French dictionary.

ALWAYS TALK IN FRANCS

When discussing how much you wish to pay, or when comparing prices, I firmly recommend you use francs. This will serve to remind you that you are buying in a foreign country, and it will iron out any fluctuations in the exchange rate that may occur while you are searching, allowing you to compare like with like. But be warned! In the last two years sterling has gone up and down against the franc like a demented yo-yo, though this should now be changing with Britain's entry into the ERM.

TRY TO SPEAK FRENCH

The French are very enthusiastic about their culture and their language, so if you show a willingness to speak French it will always be appreciated. It is not a matter of speaking fluently, more a matter of trying. It is very difficult to reject someone who is clearly trying, and you will find a ready response and an eagerness to explain to you the correct form (which, in my case, occurs quite frequently). There is another advantage in speaking French, particularly if you are careful to disguise how much you actually understand, for it often happens that the French will gabble away among themselves, assuming that the *Anglais*, or the *Rosbif*, does not understand. There is a whole new life down there.

There are evening classes that you can attend during the winter months, and also a range of programmes, cassettes and books from the BBC that are quite good. The advantage of evening classes is the possibility of meeting and swapping notes with others who are on the same obstacle course as yourself.

WHERE WILL YOU STAY?

You might now consider where you will stay while in your house-hunting area. There are two main choices: *hôtel* or a *chambre d'hôte*, which is the French equivalent of a bed and breakfast. Each has advantages. I would be inclined to argue that a *hôtel* is the most sensible for your first trip. This is not only a matter of facilities – telephones for example – but also, if you select the *hôtel* from a guide such as 'Logis de France', which is much used by visitors, there is a good chance others with the same purpose as yourself will have been there before you and the *hôtel* desk may have become quite knowledgeable on the subject of house-hunting.

The advantage of the *chambre d'hôte* is that it is usually run by local people, perhaps small farmers who have lived there for ever. In rural areas you will find they seem to know everyone and everything that is going on, which could be quite helpful. It might also be a good idea to have a local contact who could telephone you if they hear of anything of interest. And never forget that if your search is successful you will need someone locally to keep a friendly eye on your house when you are not there, and indeed someone who might be a useful contact for reliable builders, electricians, plumbers, and so on. With that thought in mind, it is a good policy to 'sleep around' a bit, clearly not in the same village or town, but as widely as possible throughout your chosen area.

Syndicats d'Initiative are a good source of names, addresses and telephone numbers of *chambres d'hôte* and local *hôtels*, and the 'Logis de France' guide is available from the French Tourist Office (Appendix E, page 85). While in the area, do not forget to use the local Yellow Pages for estate agents and *notaires*. Also, keep your eyes open for the local 'freebie' newspapers that live by advertising alone, for they are a fruitful source of properties for sale.

At this point I should mention Minitel. France Telecom are in the process of loading the telephone directories for all the *départements* of France on to a computer. Minitel is a VDU and keyboard terminal off of this computer that can be rented for a modest amount and attached to a telephone line. There is usually a Minitel or two at the main post office of most towns. Thus it is possible to search for estate agents and *notaires* simply by getting the Minitel to scroll through the relevant sections of the directory. Moreover, your search need not be limited to the particular *département* in which the town happens to be located, for, as long as the data for the *département* has been loaded on, it is possible to interrogate it from anywhere in France.

French keyboard layouts differ from those in the UK, and of course specific executive keys are identified in French. However the software is very user-friendly and it is not too difficult to discover the procedure by trial-and-error. Some post offices even display instructions in English (doubtless to avoid a repetition of earlier experiences at the hands of *Rosbifs*, who had reduced the system to a shambles, and risked a main-frame meltdown).

You will need a pencil and paper for there is no Minitel printer. Nonetheless it represents a major step forward and access to the national directory is not the only service it offers to subscribers of France Telecom.

HOW WILL YOU GET THERE AND HOW WILL YOU SEARCH?

The final point to consider at this stage is how you are going to travel, and with whom. Clearly this will be heavily influenced by the area of France in which you intend to buy and your location in the UK. What is certain is that while you are looking you are going to need a car. Flying there and hiring one is an option, but can be expensive. The alternative is to use a cross-Channel ferry and, once across, either drive the whole distance or use motorail, if a service is available. The drawback with motorail is that the service tends to be restricted to summer months and to a limited number of destinations. A list of Channel coast motorail departure points and destinations is included in Appendix L, page 95.

For the majority, the choice will be to ferry across and then to drive the whole distance. The available routes are Ramsgate/Dunkerque, Dover/Calais, Folkestone/Boulogne or Newhaven/Dieppe (south-east UK to north-east France); Portsmouth, Poole, or Weymouth/Le Havre, Caen, Cherbourg, St Malo (central UK to north/north-west France); and Plymouth/ Roscoff (west UK to north-west France). Each of these routes has its own access problems, which you will need to consider in relation to your location in the UK and your destination.

ACCESS PROBLEMS

First let us consider the problems on the UK side. The drawback of Ramsgate, Folkestone, and Dover is the need to get around London. The M25 helps, but, as I write, a 35-mile tailback is being reported because of an accident. Incidents such as this, which can rapidly choke the road, make it difficult to plan journey times. Moreover, the M2 stops well short of Dover, and the M20 to Folkestone has a nasty gap between Maidstone and Ashford. The M20 is scheduled to be completed in 1991, but the M2 will not be extended to Dover until 1997. The result is bound to mean increased delays and greater uncertainty in journey times.

Much the same can be said for Newhaven, as access from most of the country involves the M25. The M23 stops at Gatwick airport, leaving the traveller to pick a route through a maze of local roads and county towns, which in summer can be very busy with local holiday traffic.

For these reasons Ramsgate, Dover, Folkestone and New-haven are fine if you live in London, between London and Dover, or in East Anglia; for the rest of us, the alternative of Portsmouth, Poole, Weymouth/Le Havre, Caen, Cherbourg, St Malo is certainly worth considering, particularly if your destination is northern, western or south-western France.

Access to Portsmouth and Poole, which are almost but not quite at opposite ends of the M27, would be good were it not for the gap in the motorway between Winchester, where the M3 ends, and the M27. This gap is also scheduled to be closed in 1991, and this should improve access to Portsmouth, although Poole will still suffer access problems, particularly for midday arrivals and departures on summer weekends due to local holiday traffic in the Bournemouth area. Weymouth is not bad at all, especially if approached from the north or west. Plymouth also lacks the problems that so bedevil travel in the south-east.

On the French side, access seems to be a mirror-image of the UK. Dunkerque, Calais and Boulogne have autoroutes close by, but the drawback is the need to get around Paris – and the problem there is the *Périphérique*. For those who have not had the pleasure, the *Périphérique* is the M25 times two for the brio of the driving. Of course, if you are heading east and south-east, Paris can be avoided by using the A26 to Reims, but no such autoroute alternative exists if you are heading west or south-west.

Dieppe's access problems reflect those of Newhaven, for it is some 40 miles from Rouen, not the easiest of cities, and the nearest autoroute is the A13 to Paris.

Le Havre and Caen have access to this autoroute, and both are well placed for the traveller who wishes to head south but would prefer not to give the *Périphérique* a twirl. Le Havre is smaller than Caen and easier to leave, particularly if you use the *sous-terrain* to avoid the traffic lights. Be careful of your roof rack though; the clearance is not great. Caen is a big industrial city, and can be difficult to travel through, particularly in the evening rush-hour.

Cherbourg, St Malo and Roscoff are rather like Weymouth and Plymouth in that they have no autoroutes and offer ordinary roads to the south; nor are they that large.

SAILING FREQUENCIES AND CROSSING TIMES

The south-east corner of the UK packs in an enormous number of sailings per day and has by far the shortest crossing times. The Sally Line offers five sailings per day between Ramsgate and Dunkerque, with a crossing time of two-and-a-half hours. On the Dover to Calais route alone, P&O and Sealink between them offer over 30 crossings a day in August. Crossing time is one-and-a-quarter hours.

This compares very favourably with the other routes to the west, where the number of sailings is around three per day with crossing times between four and nine hours. In some instances – Portsmouth to Le Havre or Caen, for example – the combination of three departures and a six-hour crossing results in either inconveniently early departure times (08.00), inconveniently late arrival times (22.00), or the additional cost of a night cabin or hotel room on this or that side of the water.

CHOOSING THE ROUTE

While this is very much a matter of personal preference, some general guidance can be given. For example, it is perfectly possible to travel from London to Nantes via Dover, Calais, Paris and the A11. If you leave early in the morning, you will have arrived by about 20.00. Equally, it is possible to travel to Nantes via Portsmouth, St Malo and the N137. Again, if you leave early in the morning, you will have arrived by about 20.00.

My recommendation would be to travel via Portsmouth because you will encounter fewer problems than the alternative, and it would leave you in better shape for house-hunting on the following day. Your objective is to find the least stressful and most direct route. If you live in London, East Anglia, Kent or Sussex and intend to search in the Pas de Calais, near Paris, or to head south for the Alps or the Midi, then the advantages offered by the south-east England/north-east France routes are considerable. It is when your destination is La Rochelle, Tours, Brive or Bordeaux, and the point of departure Oxford, Birmingham or Manchester that Portsmouth begins to look more attractive.

From Portsmouth there are services to Le Havre, Caen, Cherbourg and St Malo. On the whole there is little to choose between Le Havre and Caen, but Le Havre is closer to Paris via the A13, and better placed to cut across-country to Orléans for Bourges and Limoges. However, in my opinion, when heading south, the roads between Caen and Le Mans are a little easier than those between Le Havre and Le Mans, and so I would recommend Caen if you are going to Le Mans to join the A11, or go beyond to Tours and join the A10 for Poitiers or Bordeaux. If you are going no further south than the Loire, it hardly matters which you choose.

What of Cherbourg? Well, routes to Cherbourg also start from Poole (four-and-a-half hours) and Weymouth (four hours), compared with the five hours from Portsmouth. However, as it takes about an hour-and-a-half to drive the length of the Cotentin Peninsula to, say, Caen and the routes to Paris or the south, these alternatives do not offer any significant advantage, and so I use Caen because the driving is minimized. Cherbourg is fine if you are searching around the peninsula or round the corner toward St Malo or in Normandy itself, but not if you are going further south than the Loire. A recent change that would have made Cherbourg competitive was the arrival of Seacat, which offered a crossing time from Portsmouth of two hours forty minutes, with five sailings each way each day. Unfortunately, having promised much, Seacat delivered nothing, at least to me, for when I arrived at Cherbourg I learned that the first Seacat was in dry-dock, and the second had not been delivered.

St Malo is well placed not only for Brittany but also Nantes and the beaches of the Vendée. The journey time from Portsmouth is nine hours, but Nantes is only two-and-a-half hours from St Malo, and the Vendée only four. I always use St Malo when I visit friends in Nantes because it is a shorter drive than to Caen. Additionally, the road from Angers to Caen is very slow, and the route through Caen from this direction to the ferry at Ouistreham is poorly signposted.

The advantages offered by St Malo peter out if your destination on the west coast reaches as far south as La Rochelle. At this point the attractions of Niort and the A10 to Tours, and then north to Caen are overwhelming. Certainly from Saintes, which is where I have my house, the A10 is excellent and the journey to Caen takes about six hours. Bordeaux is a further hour's drive to the south.

The route I have not used and the ports I do not know are Plymouth and Roscoff. The advantage of using Roscoff for Brittany is plain to see, and it is difficult to imagine anywhere in Brittany being more than three hours from the port. Moreover, the crossing time from Plymouth is only six hours, so if you are starting from the west of the UK to search in Brittany the route is most competitive.

WHICH CARRIER?

The advantage of selecting a route early is that it allows you to identify your carrier. This is important because with the Channel Tunnel on the horizon – or rather, below it – the ferry companies have started to offer discounts to regular travellers.

As ever, there are two little wrinkles to overcome: first, not all the carriers operate on every route. Ramsgate/Dunkerque is Sally Line; Dover/Calais and/or Folkestone/Boulogne are P&O, Sealink and Hoverspeed; Newhaven/Dieppe is Sealink; Portsmouth/Le Havre is P&O; Portsmouth/Caen is Brittany Ferries; Portsmouth/Cherbourg is P&O and Sealink; Poole/

Cherbourg is Brittany Ferries; Weymouth/Cherbourg is Sea-link; Portsmouth/St Malo is Brittany Ferries; and finally, Plymouth/Roscoff is Brittany Ferries. Thus P&O and Sealink do not cross the Channel west of Cherbourg, and Brittany Ferries do not cross it east of Caen, unless something goes terribly, terribly wrong!

The second wrinkle is that not all of the routes are open the whole year round. Those that do *not* run the whole year are Poole/Cherbourg, which runs between May and September only; Portsmouth/St Malo, between March and December; and P&O Portsmouth/Cherbourg, which runs from mid-March to mid-December only.

Finally, what are the incentives that are being showered upon us? They are of two sorts. Brittany Ferries has the Property Owners' Club, which you can join *once* you have bought your house. It offers discounts of up to 30 percent on travel costs and certain meals, and you get a discount on travel costs when you make your booking. There is an entrance fee of £25 and an annual fee of £15. At first glance the obvious response is to travel with the others and not use Brittany Ferries until you can enjoy the perks. However, Brittany Ferries offer a range of 'go as you please' motoring holidays, which include the ferry fare and vouchers for accommodation at selected two-star hotels. These are very much the sort of hotel you will find in the 'Logis de France' which I recommended earlier, and using the holiday package could be a significant economy. The key is the distribution of selected hotels and their relevance to your search area. I have found it is not necessary to stay in one of the hotels every night as hoteliers in the selected hotels are happy to accept unused accommodation vouchers as payment for meals.

With P&O the scheme allows points to be accumulated which are then used as discounts against future fares by 20 percent. This, however, requires sending in a claim by post to get the discount, which can then be applied to the next fare. The Sealink scheme works in a similar way, and also offers a 20 percent discount. In both cases it is necessary to join a club, but there is no entrance fee or annual subscription.

SUMMARY

- Maps
- *Syndicat d'Initiative*
- Bank accounts
- The house
- Always talk in francs
- Try to speak French
- Where will you stay
- How will you get there and how will you search?
- Access problems
- Sailing frequencies and crossing times
- Choosing the route
- Which carrier?

PART TWO

BUYING IT

INTRODUCTION

Well now, here we are: paradise found, dream house located. What happens next? My advice is to take a leaf from the French approach to life and find a restaurant. This is a prudent step, firstly because little good comes from decisions made on an empty stomach; secondly because you will need somewhere to sit and rehearse the questions you will need to ask; thirdly because if it is lunch-time everybody else will be eating anyway.

Once you have found the restaurant, do not rush towards the questions listed in the next chapter. Be prudent and begin by ordering an *apéritif* and follow this by deciding which menu and wine you prefer. Champagne should definitely not be ordered at this stage. Not until the *terrine du chef* has been safely dispatched and the *truite aux amandes* has been placed before you should you turn to the list of questions, for only then will you be fortified sufficiently to consider whether your dream house is a dream house after all. Disappointment is best handled on a full stomach.

CHAPTER FOUR

QUESTIONS YOU WILL NEED TO ASK

SERVICES

Does your house have town water, electricity, sewage disposal, telephone and gas? These are all things that might be covered in the information supplied, but there is no harm in double-checking with the owner. After all, the agent cannot be held responsible, and so on and so forth . . .

WATER

Take water for example. If it is not town water, it may come from your own well – but then it also may come from somebody else's well. So whose well *does* it come from? And if it is from another person's well, what are the charges, what are the arrangements for maintenance, and who pays for repairs? Does anyone have rights (*le droit de puisage*) over your water?

A final important point is, whether it is your well or not, is the water drinkable? If you wish to be assured that the water is not supplied with added protein in the form of minute animal organisms, you will need to take a sample to the local chemist

(a sample of the well water that is!). If the water is not drinkable, you will need to consider the cost of alternatives, such as getting town water connected to your house from the nearest practical point. The local water authority or company will be listed in the telephone directory, and they may be willing to give you an estimate. Alternatively, the *notaire* or seller may know their local representative, or the *mairie* may help (as a general rule, the smaller the place the more helpful the *mairie*).

ELECTRICITY

It is easy enough to see if power cables are fixed to your house. If the house is remote and no power cables and/or pylons are visible, you will need to check with *Electricité de France* on the nearest lines available and the cost of connection. Use the telephone directory, *notaire*, seller and *mairie* – the same approach as suggested for water.

SEWAGE

If there is no mains drainage and sewage then you will have either a hole in the ground, called a lost well, or a closed tank or a septic tank. You will need to establish which, and if a septic or closed tank needs to be installed, or the house connected to the town system, you will again need estimates. This time the *mairie* is the best source of names of contractors and local artisans.

TELEPHONE

Telephone cables are easy to spot. In France, if there is a cable you are connected automatically upon buying a house, so there is nothing more to do. If, however, there is no cable and one will be needed you will have to confirm the cost. The simplest way of getting an estimate is to dial 14 and ask. Although *France Telecom* is not keen on giving estimates to someone who does not own the house, they can be cajoled and persuaded to give a rough figure.

GAS

If the town has no gas that is the end of the matter. If there is gas in the town but it is not connected, again you will need an estimate. Gas is usually supplied by *Electricité de France*, the same people who supply the electricity.

THE CONDITION OF THE HOUSE

If your house or *appartement* is new or of modern construction, little should need to be done apart from decoration. If, however, it is an old house, then the older it is the more likely it is that repairs and restoration will be necessary. Assuming, then, that the house is of a certain age:

THE OUTSIDE

What are the tiles like? Do they form a straight line, or are they ragged, uneven or broken?

Is the roof line clean and straight? Or does it sag and bend?

Does the house have gutters and down-pipes? If so, are they in good condition? Is there any indication that the gutters leak, or that the down-pipes overflow? Are there damp marks on the stonework?

Are the shutters and doors sound? Are they strong or weak on their hinges?

Does the land round about the house flood? How high is the water level in winter?

Are there any rights of way?

Is there an advertising hoarding on the house or on your land? Publicity contracts run for the life of the contract, and are not affected by a change of ownership.

INSIDE

Can you smell damp? Do the walls feel damp? Is the paper hanging loose?

Do the timbers suffer from wet or dry rot? Does your car key slide into the beam with little resistance? Are there beetle holes? Little piles of sawdust?

What about the floors? Do they give as you walk across? Does your foot go through the floor? (I should mention that no gentleman allows his wife to cross the floor first).

Tap the plaster – is it still adhering firmly to the wall, or does it sound hollow?

What about the wiring? Is it up to modern standards? How many points are there?

How hard does it freeze in winter? Is the heating good enough? Is there any insulation on water pipes or in the roof?

SUMMARY

- Services
- Water
- Electricity
- Sewage
- Telephone
- Gas
- The condition of the house (outside, inside)

CHAPTER FIVE

THE OFFER

By now you should be approaching the end of your meal and nicely psyched-up for the struggle to come. There is not a lot we can do to help you except to point out a few French formalities.

INHERITANCE

In France inheritance laws are rather different from those in the UK, so it is perhaps timely to touch upon them while you savour your *digestif* and before you commit yourself to a purchase.

Put simply, upon your death French law gives your relatives rights over your property. Put another way, your freedom to leave your assets to whomsoever you jolly-well wish is severely curtailed. Thus, if you have children they are entitled to between half and three-quarters of your estate, depending on how many of them there are.

This restriction is not limited to children. In France, if *le défunt* (the deceased) has no issue, then brothers and sisters have rights, which can extend upwards to parents in the event that *le défunt* has no brothers and sisters and no issue.

Of course this will apply only to that part of your estate that is based in France, if your house is to be a holiday home and you intend to remain a resident of the UK, only the French house and land will be subject to French law. Other items that are owned and that may have been in France at the time of death, furniture, or your Canalettos, for example, will be subject to the law of the land in which you are resident, namely the UK, and you will be free to leave them to the Battersea Dogs Home if that is your wish.

It follows that if you become a resident of France, then your French house, land, goods and chattels both in France and elsewhere become subject to French law. If you had retained a property in the UK only that property would be subject to UK law, but the furniture or the cash that was there would be subject to French law.

The most curious aspect of inheritance law in France is that while children, brothers, sisters, Uncle Tom Cobley and all might have rights, the surviving half of a couple (*conjoint survivant*) seems to have no rights other than that of usage of the property for his or her lifetime.

Of course none of this may be of any concern to you. French law may be no more than you intended anyway; after all, in the UK it is perfectly possible to leave an estate to children, but to give the surviving spouse the use for his/her lifetime.

If, however, it is of concern, there are steps that can be taken to ameliorate the position. First, obviously, buy the property jointly so that only half of it is affected by the death of one spouse. Next, ensure that any part of the estate that is not subject to reserved portions is cross-willed to the surviving spouse to provide maximum leverage. Another is to adjust your UK will to redress any imbalance. Finally, it is possible to buy through the medium of a non-resident company, and avoid the problem. I must confess, however, I am uneasy about the latter, and it should be done only after the greatest possible thought and with legal advice.

Should you be interested in reading up on the matter I recommend the Institut Français in South Kensington, where you should ask for the library and then for the Dalloz Code Civil which explains French inheritance law. You will find them most amiable and co-operative, even providing free photocopies of their material.

FEES AND TAXES

In France the purchaser pays the fees for negotiating the sale – for example, the estate agent's fee if there is one (or the *notaire*'s fee where a *notaire* has acted in the role of estate agent), plus taxes, stamp duty, land registry fees and expenses. The purchaser also pays the fee due to the *notaire* for the conveyancing of the property – local search certificate, enquiries into local planning considerations, and establishing there is no charge or mortgage in existence, which is obligatory for the transfer of property.

These costs can amount to 18 percent of the cost of the house, and are in addition to the price of the property, but often it is not clear whether they are included in the price or not. It is therefore essential to establish what is or is not included in the price before making an offer.

On the whole, if you are buying direct from the owner it is likely that no costs will be included and you will have to pay the *notaire* separately for the conveyancing and the taxes. If you are buying through an estate agent the entire 18 percent may already be included in the asking price. Or perhaps only the estate agent's fees are, in which case you will have to settle separately with the *notaire* for the conveyancing and the taxes. Or perhaps nothing at all has been added; just be careful and make sure.

As a matter of course, always offer below the asking price even if it says *prix firme et définitif* (you can always use the language barrier to your advantage when you have to). Confirm any price offered in writing, and if the price offered is substantially below the asking price because of the condition of the house, it always helps to attach a list of the things that need to be done, with, where possible, estimates of the costs.

NOTAIRE

If your offer is accepted, the next step is to sign an agreement called a *compromis*. To do that you will need a *notaire*. If you are buying through a *notaire* you will not have far to look, if you are buying through an estate agent he will most certainly know of one, and if you are buying direct you can use the seller's or go to the Yellow Pages or to Minitel.

The *notaire* is a sort of semi-public official, whose job is to ensure that the conveyance of the property is done properly and the state gets its cut, i.e. its taxes, or *impots*. Therefore, it is the custom for the *notaire* to represent both parties, and so the adversarial approach of the UK system with solicitors representing each party does not exist.

The difficulty is that the documentation will all be in French, and obviously it is prudent to understand what it is you are being asked to sign. You will need to arrange to have a translation made. This may not be as difficult as it sounds, and the larger the place the more likely you are to find an interpreter. Try Minitel, the *mairie* or the *Syndicat d'Initiative*. Alternatively, the documents could be brought back to the UK and translated here. Or, you could return to the adversarial system and get a UK solicitor to handle the matter (there are many who advertise in the overseas property press). On the whole I favour using the *notaire* and getting a translation, as the local *notaire* is going to know a jolly sight more of local conditions than a UK solicitor.

COMPROMIS

If your offer is accepted, the next step is to sign an agreement called a *compromis*. This is not essential, but it does eliminate any possibility of gazumping, being binding on both buyer and seller.

Make sure that under the part labelled *Situation et Désignation* there is the fullest possible description of the property – main dwelling, outbuildings, land, garden, number of rooms, central heating – everything of significance, even trees and shrubs if they are of particular importance.

Although binding, the *compromis* automatically contains two suspensive clauses that offer the buyer protection against unforeseen happenings:

Le certificat d'urbanisme (a local search), which will establish if there are any developments planned for your land. But please note, only for *your* land. If the TGV route is at the bottom of the garden on someone else's land, the search may not mention it.

Right of pre-emption, which is a right reserved for the town council or the farmers' union (depending on the current use of the land) to buy for itself. The reason for the pre-emption is to ensure that no secret deals are done to save taxes, which are all percentages of the sale price, by quoting the official price low and having under-the-table payments to make up the difference. The right allows the town council to buy at the stated price. You have been warned!

There is always space on the *compromis* form for a third suspensive clause, and if your purchase is dependent upon raising a mortgage, it is prudent to ensure that this third clause is in respect to your ability to raise the finance. In fact, there is no limit to the number of suspensive clauses you can have,

No M'sieur – I do not think it is a DAM. – In any case – you will not see it for the pretty trees!

43

and if there are understandings between you and the seller, for example, you will buy at 'X' if he will repair the roof, or get water connected, or for any other condition, get it added to the *compromis*. They may not like it, but get it in.

With the *compromis* it is usual to pay a deposit of 10 percent of the agreed price of the house or *appartement*. This is not, however, obligatory. In my own case I was asked neither for a deposit nor to sign a *compromis*.

It is possible to sign the *compromis* first and send the money for the deposit over from the UK later. It may also be possible for you to be sent the *compromis* to sign in the UK if you return before your offer has been accepted. Another alternative is to issue a power of attorney to, say, the *notaire*'s clerk, who will sign the *compromis* on your behalf. If you intend to do this it is better to sign the attorney in France at the *notaire*'s office; if you sign in the UK you will have to get it ratified by the French Consul General, which takes time and is a nuisance.

After the *compromis* has been signed, allow a minimum of six weeks for the *notaire* to make the searches, although this can be much reduced if the searches have been done ahead of the sale.

MORTGAGES

In France it is not possible to get an agreement for a mortgage until you have made an offer for a property that has been accepted, and a *compromis* has been signed. Nor is it possible to obtain a mortgage for more than 80 percent of the value of a property. If it is an old property in need of extensive repairs, the 80 percent can apply to the purchase price plus the cost of repairs. Estimates must be supplied and invoices provided as the money is given as the work progresses. It *is* possible to fiddle the figures by encouraging workmen to inflate the level of estimates and the price of invoices. It is not unheard of for estate agents to offer to inflate the book price of the property. All these practices are extremely risky, not to say illegal, and are *not* recommended for an *étranger* buying in a foreign country.

If you need a mortgage in France you will need to be able

to supply evidence of your income and your ability to repay the loan. Since changes were made to the convertibility of the French franc in 1989, the growth of the range of mortgages available has been phenomenal. It is now possible to raise money in sterling to be repaid in sterling, sterling to be repaid in francs, and francs to be repaid in sterling.

I touched on the volatility of the franc/sterling exchange rate earlier when I advised always to consider the price of a house in francs. This volatility is entirely a product of the relative strength of sterling. For example, the Ff/DM rate has fluctuated round a margin of three percent since February 1988, whereas the Ff/£ rate has moved about ten percent above and below 10.00 over the same period. Now, on entry to the ERM, it is back up at 10.08.

It has been argued that Britain's entry to the ERM will stabilize these fluctuations. I have no doubt it will damp them down, but with a feeling abroad that the pound will need to fall by 15 percent if the balance of payments deficit is to be corrected, it is perfectly possible to imagine the pound slipping below its permitted range of six percent and dropping as low as 9.00–9.10. Nor is there anything in the arrangements of the ERM to prevent this happening. It will not be called a devaluation of course, but a realignment. There have been 14 such realignments since the ERM was launched in 1979, and there is no reason to suppose there will not be more.

The question of a franc mortgage needs to be considered against the background I have outlined above. For, although a 10½ percent mortgage rate has its attractions when the UK rate is 15 percent, this differential is soon eroded if the pound begins to fall. Consider the following example where Ff110,000 are borrowed. At a Ff/£ rate of 11.00 the sterling equivalent is £10,000. However, if the Ff/£ rate falls from 11.00 to 10.00, the sterling equivalent rises to £11,000. Not only will the sterling equivalent of the sum borrowed rise, but also the monthly payments. A monthly payment of Ff1,000 will cost £100, where the Ff/£ rate is 10.00. If, however, the rate falls to 9.00, the monthly cost of the Ff1,000 will be £111. It is therefore perfectly possible to envisage a situation where, despite a year of increased payments, you will find that your debt in sterling terms has actually risen.

Of course if you have a franc income none of these exchange

rate considerations need worry you. But if you do not, and will dependent on transferring sums monthly, my advice would be to think long and hard before committing yourself to a franc mortgage. Do not forget that your mortgage will run for more than a year or two, and whatever you decide, only use reputable sources.

Once all the searches are completed and show no substantial impediment to your purchase, and once you have the finance, the next step is the *acte de vente*.

ACTE DE VENTE

This is the document that will effect the sale. It is important to have either an interpreter on hand when you go to sign it, or to have a copy sent to the UK where it can be translated and where you can get legal advice, or both.

It is essential to make sure that every point covered in your agreement is present in the 'Charge and Conditions' section of the *acte de vente*: rights of way, rights of access to water, ownership of walls, gutters, downpipes, and so on. Make sure they are all included, and make sure that the searches by the *notaire* have not produced any substantial problems of which you were unaware and which may prevent your proceeding with the purchase. Do not forget that you will be signing to the effect that you are buying the buildings as seen, that is, exactly as they are. Nor should you forget that you will be accepting all rights (*servitudes* in French), which will include payment of land taxes, etc., gas, water, electricity charges, and that you will pay all state taxes arising from your purchase.

Make sure too that the house has a certificate in regard to termite infection. Termites are not a problem in the UK but they are a considerable menace in France; the French regard the death-watch beetle as benign in comparison to the termite.

When you sign the *acte de vente*, and initial every page of it, you will need to hand over the balance of the money owed, either in the form of a banker's draft or a cheque drawn on a French bank account. Have nothing to do with any under-the-table payments, for you will sign in recognition that everything is declared.

The taxes levied will be less if the house is for your own use. In which case, you must not let the house for a period of three years, not even for a day. If you do let the house and the tax people get to hear of it, the higher rate of tax will be payable.

While on the subject of taxation, let us turn briefly to income tax and capital gains tax insofar as they affect your house. There is a Double Taxation Agreement between France and the UK. Details can be obtained from:

> Direction Générale des Impôts
> Centre des Impôts des Non-résidents
> 9, rue d'Uzes
> 75094 PARIS CEDEX 02

You should write to that address and inform them that you have bought a house and give its address. They will send you a useful document which sets out the steps that should be taken in a variety of different circumstances. As you might expect, any net letting income is subject to tax and must be declared. Captial gains tax also applies to any profit accruing from the sale of the house. Expenses incurred in renovating, restoring and repairing the house are allowed against the profit, so make sure you keep the bills for any work done. And finally, when you leave the *notaire*'s office, make sure you take the keys.

Congratulations! You may now open the champagne.

SUMMARY

- Inheritance
- Fees and taxes
  - *Notaire*
  - *Compromis*
  - Mortgages
  - *Acte de vente*

PART THREE

MOVING IN

CHAPTER SIX

TAKING OVER

So, you have signed the *acte de vente*, handed over the money, and received the keys in return. So what now?

First, you will need to get the services transferred to your name and working. If the house has been occupied this is relatively easy. The probability that the seller was at the *notaire*'s bureau with you is high and, indeed, may well leave at the same time and with the same intention as you – namely to transfer the services into your name and to read the meters.

SERVICES – HOUSE OCCUPIED

WATER

Mains water is metered in France, so it will be necessary to read the meter. A telephone call is then sufficient to get the change made. Do not forget to give your UK address for billing if you are not going to be resident. Bills can be paid by cheque, and standing orders and direct debit facilities are also available – but remember that these will be on your French bank account. As the seller will also wish to advise the water company that he will no longer be the user, it may be that a single telephone call will suffice.

ELECTRICITY AND GAS

Once again, it is a matter of reading the meters and making the change. Give your UK address for bills if you are not going to be resident. Payment can be made by cheque, and standing orders and direct debit are also available.

TELEPHONE

Dial 14 and ask for the transfer. They will need to know the name of your predecessor. Do not forget to give them your UK address for bills if you are not going to be resident. Similar payment arrangements exist as for electricity and gas.

SERVICES – HOUSE UNOCCUPIED

When the house has been unoccupied or some of the services are missing, things may not be as straightforward. There may not, for example, be anyone at the *notaire*'s bureau if the sale is on behalf of executors. In this case it will be back to basics. Before you leave the *notaire*, make sure you get the telephone numbers and addresses for those services you need to contact – or go and ask at the *mairie* immediately.

WATER

If the water is cut off you will need to find the meter. If there is a meter, read it, turn on the water, and proceed as described earlier. If there is no meter, you will need to telephone for an appointment for a new meter to be installed. You will need to have francs or a French cheque when the meter is installed as payment is expected on the spot. This is not expensive – mine cost around Ff200.

If there is no mains water and you have your own well water that is drinkable, all you need be concerned with is that the pump works once you have switched on the electricity. If you are drawing water from someone else's well, you will need to let them know and make arrangements about payment.

ELECTRICITY AND GAS

If the electricity and gas have not been disconnected, all you will have to do is throw a switch and proceed as described earlier. If there has been a disconnection, it will be necessary to write to EDF requesting an appointment for reconnection. (see Appendix K, page 94).

TELEPHONE

If there is a socket but no phone you will need to know the name of the person who lived there previously. You can get this from the *acte de vente* or from the *notaire*. Dial 14 from the nearest payphone or from your hotel and ask to be connected. If there is no phone, no socket, and no indication of a line, you will need to order one. Follow the same procedure as for connection. A new line with two sockets and one phone costs about Ff500.

INSURANCE

In the *acte de vente* it is your responsibility from day one to insure the property. A number of options are available: you could ask the seller if you could continue with his insurance; you could ask the *notaire* to recommend an insurer; you could try the Yellow Pages; or, ask your French bank for a recommendation.

SUMMARY

- Services – house occupied
  - Water
  - Electricity and gas
  - Telephone
- Services – house unoccupied
  - Water
  - Electricity and gas
  - Telephone
  - Insurance

CHAPTER SEVEN

REPAIRS, RENOVATIONS AND RESTORATION

PLANNING PERMISSION

If your intention is simply to repair or to make good and then to decorate, replacing the wiring, for example, or the plumbing, you will not need planning permission. For more major works, however, you will need it. If you intend road- or pavement-side works such as fencing, you will require a *demande d'alignement* from the *mairie*. Moving up a stage to, say, an opening for a window or a door, you will require a *demande de travaux sans permis de construire*. And if you intend major works such as additions above 20m² (215 sq ft) or a change of use – converting a barn into a habitable dwelling, for example – full planning permission is essential.

BUILDERS AND TRADESMEN

To locate help, use the Yellow Pages and the local newspapers. The *mairie* may well be a good source of names. On the whole

it is politic to use local people, as putting money into the local economy is better than not, and it will also help to establish your credentials and place in the community.

SUPERVISION OF BUILDING WORKS

If you do not intend to do the work yourself, you will need someone you can trust to oversee the work. *Maîtres d'oeuvre* are listed in the Yellow Pages, and charge around three percent of the cost. Make sure you keep the bills.

PAYMENT FOR WORK DONE

In France it is customary to pay a percentage of the cost when the estimate is agreed to allow for the purchase of materials. As in the UK, people will often take less if paid in cash – but then you may not get a receipt.

SUMMARY

- Planning permission
- Builders and tradesmen
- Supervision of building works
- Payment for work done

SOMEBODY YOU CAN TRUST TO OVERSEE THE WORK.

CHAPTER EIGHT

THE MOVE

TRANSFERRING HOUSEHOLD EFFECTS

This is not a simple question of moving goodies you own from one house to another, but of *exporting* from the UK and *importing* into France. It is sensible to approach this from two points of view: moving the goodies, or, as HM Customs and Excise will have it, the 'household effects', from the UK to France, and then returning them.

UK TO FRANCE – THE UK SIDE

On a first approach, HM Customs and Excise will maintain they have no interest in UK citizens shipping their household effects to France unless these include banned substances such as Semtex or crack. So if you intend to ship these to France, do not forget to tell HM Customs. For your favourite wardrobe, however, all you have to do is to take it.

A time may come, however, when you decide you would prefer to have your favourite wardrobe back in the UK rather than in France. Then, of course, you will be *importing* into the UK. You will need to prove that duty and tax were paid, and a copy of the out-going inventory will be invaluable.

UK TO FRANCE – FRENCH SIDE

The French Embassy is very used to telephone calls from British people asking how to ship household effects to France. You will be directed to the junior branch, the Consulate General (located at 21 Cromwell Road, London SW7 2EN, far removed from the splendours of Grosvenor Square) with commendable efficiency and not a little disdain. After all, who wants *les grandes affaires d'état* contaminated with your grotty wardrobe?

The Consulate General is also used to such enquiries, and you will soon find yourself listening to a tape recording explaining what you must do if you *really do* wish to ship your goods to France.

Listening to the tape, you will realize that the first thing you will need to decide is whether you are going to become a resident in France, or whether you are going to remain a resident of the UK, and use your house in France as a holiday home only. You may well have decided this before you even bought this book, in which case it is simply a matter of following the relevant directions. For those of us who keep changing our minds, or who have not even made up our minds, another problem emerges. Notwithstanding the fact that it is listing all the important requirements you will need to satisfy French Customs, the tape will proceed at such a pace that unless you are capable of 100 wpm shorthand, you will have to listen to it again. The relief you experience when you discover that the tape is on a loop will soon be replaced by your distress when you realize that it is accelerating relentlessly, until the voice is little more than a high-pitched gabble (I have a vision of some faceless *fonctionnaire* ruthlessly tweaking up the speed).

PERMANENT RESIDENCE

As I have persevered and lived to tell the tale, I can tell you that if you are going to reside permanently in France, your household effects will need to be accompanied by the following:

- Evidence of your residence in the UK, which must specify the length of time you have been living there. This can be a statement from an officer of your local authority, a JP, or a solicitor.

- Documentary evidence of your residence in France. A copy of your *acte de vente* should suffice.

- A photocopy of the first five pages of your passport.

- Either a contract of employment for France or a *visa d'établissement* if you are an EC national not intending to work in France or set up a commercial or industrial business.

- Two original copies of a detailed inventory, in French, valued in French francs, for each item, including vehicles. This should carry an assurance that the goods have been owned for three months in the case of household effects, and six months for vehicles, and will not be disposed of within 12 months of the date of importation.

Finally, if you live in the south of England the necessary documents can be obtained by writing to: PO Box 57, French Consulate General, 21 Cromwell Road, London SW7 2EN. Include a large stamped, self-addressed envelope. If you live in the north, the address is: French Consulate General, 523/535 Cunard Building, Pier Head, Liverpool L3 1ET; if living in Scotland write to: French Consulate General, 11 Randolph Crescent, Edinburgh EH3 7TT. Northern Ireland comes under Liverpool. Do not ask me why, ask the Consul General if you must.

The *visa d'établissement* takes over 16 weeks to acquire, and requires no less than six copies of an official form for each person who is changing their residence from the UK to France, and an interview with everyone as well.

It is also necessary to attach to each copy of the documentation:

- An affidavit affirming you do not have a criminal history, nor have you been bankrupt.

- A letter from your bank, solicitor, or accountant confirming your capital value and income.
- The title of ownership of the property in France.
- A passport photo.

For a couple, that means 12 copies of each item. The *visa d'établissement* is the most time-consuming of the items you will need, and should therefore be addressed first.

Once you have ploughed your way through the bureaucracy, matters become a little more straightforward and your household effects can be shipped without more ado. There is no limit to the number of individual shipments providing they all occur within 12 months of the date of your changing residence, and providing that a complete inventory is handed to French customs at the port of entry that shows the different consignments. The same port of entry must be used for all consignments.

The only items you will not be permitted to import into France free of tax are:

- alcoholic drinks in excess of 50 bottles, of which no more than 15 can exceed 22 deg Gay Lussac;
- tobacco;
- commercial vehicles;
- professional equipment;
- items less than three months old;
- vehicles less than six months old.

STATE PENSION, HEALTH COVERAGE, DRIVER'S LICENCE

Finally, do not forget to check on the effect your departure may have on your state pension. This is particularly important if you have retired at 60 and are not yet drawing a state pension, as the years between 60 and 65 are only credited if you are a resident in the UK. Do not forget to complete Form E111 to secure reciprocal health coverage; and do not forget that when resident in France you will need a French driving licence.

NON-RESIDENT SECONDARY HOME

If you do not intend to reside permanently in France, and intend to use your house as a second home and for holiday purposes, a different set of regulations applies. To begin with, the list of items you cannot import tax-free is more extensive:

- tobacco;
- alcoholic drinks;
- food stocks;
- motor vehicles (cars, motorbikes, mopeds, aeroplanes);
- boats, caravans, mobile homes;
- tools currently used for the maintenance or fitting up of the residence;
- anything less than three months old.

You will need to provide French customs with three copies of:

- A completed application form, which will include a declaration that you will not dispose of the items, nor sell, let or loan the residence for 12 months after the date of the importation.
- A detailed inventory in French and valued in French francs.
- A proof of ownership or tenancy of the property, such as an *attestation notariée* or an *attestation de loueur*.
- Proof of your permanent residence in the UK (see above).

To obtain the necessary documentation write to: PO Box 520 at the French Consulate General in London if you live in the south of England and the Midlands. You will need to supply a large, stamped, addressed envelope, and indicate which *département* your holiday home is located in as this will determine the regional customs office to which your application must be submitted. Those living in other areas of the UK should apply to the appropriate addresses listed on page 59 above.

The procedure is straightforward:

- Write and request the documentation;
- Complete the forms and send them to the customs office indicated;
- Wait for the arrival of the authorization, which takes about a month and will include a stamped copy of your inventory;
- Load up and head for France, and when you get there produce the authorization and the stamped copy of the inventory.

As with permanent residence you can take more than one consignment, providing the inventory lists the various consignments and providing you use the same port of entry every time.

SHIPPERS

Of course you do not have to make the move yourself as there are many shippers who specialize in moving household effects to France. It pays to shop around, and I have found fees not to be excessive when compared to the cost of hiring a large van and doing it yourself.

If you use a shipper, he will complete many of the formalities for you, but not of course your application for a *visa d'établissement*.

Remember though that they are *your* household effects and you will carry the can for any errors and omissions. Use the information given above to ensure that everything is done properly. And above all, mark and label everything thoroughly, particularly if you are sending a part load. Do not forget: *Q*. 'Where are you travelling to, Sir?' *A*. 'New York.' *Q*. 'Thank you, Sir. And where would you like your luggage to be sent?'

BUYING FURNITURE IN FRANCE

If you are furnishing a second home, it is possible you may not have spare beds, freezers and cookers lying around just waiting to be shipped to France. It may be that there is not much sense in shipping a well-used washing machine to France in any case as servicing may prove difficult in the event of a breakdown. A more sensible move might to be to dispose of older items in the UK and buy new in France. After all, shipping to France is not going to be cheap.

In my experience, the only furnishing items that are more expensive in France than in the UK are electric kettles, telephones, hi-fis, radios and VCRs. As far as the VCRs are concerned, the French TV system (SECAM, which stands for *Système Extraordinaire Contre les Américains*) differs from the UK system, so there is hardly any point in taking the VCR unless you are taking the TV and a supply of videos as well. Other items such as fridges, freezers, cookers, washing machines, irons and vacuum cleaners are the same price or cheaper. I am not talking of the prices you may find in the little shop on the corner, but prices in the major hypermarkets such as Leclerc, Intermarche, Carrefour, Rond Point and more specialist furniture suppliers such as Conforama. You will generally find these on the outskirts of towns, often grouped conveniently close together in *centres commerciaux*.

As in the UK it pays to shop around and to exploit sales where possible. Often stores have promotions or sales on the anniversary of their opening or establishment, so it is important to keep your eyes open for sales, and not just at the traditional times.

As I am not too keen on modern French furniture, and as my house is over 100 years old, I have been searching the antique dealers and junk-shops, which I have found to be expensive. Not so the sale rooms. If you want older, used furniture my recommendation is to try the *hôtels de vente*. Most large towns will have at least one, and they will be listed in the Yellow Pages and on Minitel. You may also find the local *Syndicat d'Initiative* willing to supply names and addresses.

Finally I should briefly touch upon the decoration and flooring of your house. Tiles wood and carpets are cheaper in France, but paint most certainly is not, being about twice the price you would expect to pay in the UK. Even ICI paints, which are sold under the Valentin label, are twice as expensive in France as in England.

SUMMARY

- Transferring household effects
- UK to France – the UK side
- UK to France – the France side
- Permanent residence
- State pension, health coverage, driver's licence
- Non-resident secondary home
- Shippers
- Buying furniture in France

PART FOUR

LOOKING BACK

CHAPTER NINE

REFLECTIONS

Having written about the general points to bear in mind when buying a house in France I thought it might be of use if I briefly described my own experience and tried to give some idea of the timescales involved.

My search for a house in France began seriously at Easter 1988. It was not until December 1988 that the house was located, in May 1989 the purchase was completed and it was only in Easter 1990 that I was able, even partially, to move in. In reflecting on the process I have added two further factors – travel route and being there – to the familiar three: finding it, buying it and moving in.

FINDING IT

The search began at the Ile de Noirmoutier, which is located close to the mouth of the Loire and around one-and-a-half hours' drive from Nantes. I started there because I had friends in Nantes and had often holidayed on the island. Buying on the French Channel coast was immediately eliminated as an option, as the climate there is too similar to that of southern UK.

Equally, the Biscay coast of Brittany had also been ruled out as the climate there is not significantly more reliable than that of the Channel coast. At the same time, for a number of reasons,

I did not wish to go too far south: the cost and travelling time were too great, the rising pollution of the Mediterranean and the high summer heat in the far south, which might become intolerable if global warming occurs.

However, I did want to be near a coast because it is nice to have a sea to mess about in and because its proximity would help limit the heat in summer and the cold in winter. What I did not know was how far south it would be necessary to go to find a climate which would give a reasonable extension to summer from Easter to Bonfire Night. On that basis the area between the mouth of the Loire and the mouth of the Gironde seemed a likely prospect. Thus, when the search began, the 'quarter' was established and the search targeted on the Atlantic coastline of the Vendée and Charente Maritime *départements*.

The objective was to find somewhere nice 20 to 30 miles inland from reasonable beaches and/or resorts. I began by driving south from Noirmoutier and scouring the coast for suitable places. I made three or four expeditions of seven to ten days each to do this. That duration brings the best offers from most ferry operators and, secondly, ten days of continual driving and searching is about as much as anyone can take without becoming too jaded to choose sensibly and too tired to drive safely.

When searching that hard, it is important to have a reliable guide to hotels in the area, as a good evening meal and a good night's sleep are essential. I always used the 'Logis de France' and have no complaints whatever about their standards and service. My general daily plan was to arrive at my hotel about five or six in the evening, relax and plan my search for the following day. In the morning many hotels will fill a flask with coffee for you and phone ahead to the hotel where you plan to stay that night to reserve a room for you.

I suppose I must have driven every kilometre of the coast roads of the Vendée and during the search I looked at the resorts of St Jean-de-Monts, St Gilles-Croix de Vie, Bretignolles-sur-Mer, Les Sables-D'Olonne, Jard-sur-Mer, St Vincent-sur-Jard and La Tranche-sur-Mer. At the same time, I visited the inland towns of Legé, Challans, La Roche-sur-Yon, Chantonnay, Fontenay-le-Comte and Luçon.

At each place, I took time to have a good walk around, to look in the windows of the local estate agents and *notaires* to see what was on offer and what price was being asked. Naturally, I obtained their names, addresses and telephone numbers and searched out copies of the local 'freebie' newspaper in any of the places which seemed to be of interest.

There is some lovely countryside in the Vendée, the beaches at La Tranche, for example, are beautiful, while the wooded hills around Mervent and Vouvant contrast sharply with the fenland of the Marais Poitevin. However, the climate I sought had not yet materialized and so I kept on heading south.

Now I am sure that many people who have driven south across France will have noticed a series of distinct temperature thresholds. There is one on the south side of the Channel, for example, another is to be found on the Loire and a third, I discovered, lies approximately along the line of the Sèvre river between La Rochelle and Niort. Once that line is crossed, and one leaves the Vendée for Charente Maritime, the climate feels distinctly softer. When I arrived in St Jean-d'Angély in November 1988 and found many trees still in leaf, people ambling about in shirt sleeves and the geraniums in the garden of the *Hôtel de la Paix* in full bloom, I knew I had arrived.

Finding the house once the area was identified took less than a month, for the area being searched was not large. Indeed, the house I chose is located within ten miles of St Jean. It was an intensive operation which made use of estate agents, *notaires* and local newspapers.

What was depressing though was the amount of rubbish on offer. Together with the unreliability of estate agents' descriptions, this made the final stage a heady mixture of excitement and disappointment. This may, in part, have been because I was aiming at the lower end of the market, having budgeted for an expenditure of £35,000. Nonetheless, there is a lot of rubbish about and considerable determination is required to continue searching in the face of repeated setbacks.

On the whole, I found that *notaires* who offered a property service had better-informed and more helpful staff than their equivalents who worked for estate agents. An annoying aspect of buying property through each though is that they insist on accompanying you to look at the house. Often a glance at the surroundings is enough to send one reaching for the blue pencil, but when telephone calls have been made and a rendezvous agreed it seems churlish to reject something without getting out of the car. So one finds oneself, out of politeness, wasting scarce time looking at obviously unsuitable houses. It would be preferable (and quicker) to be given their list and thus eliminate those houses located on flight paths, next to motorways or underneath water towers simply by driving past without stopping. However, that is the way the French seem to do it, so you will need to allow for that in your planning.

BUYING IT

Compared to the search, buying the house was straightforward. The first step was to arrange for my wife to visit and decide if she liked it. This was done in January 1989. Although the house was supplied with electricity and piped water, it needed restoration and therefore I needed rough estimates of the likely cost, which were easily obtained from local people. These were incorporated, that same month when I made my first offer, into a letter to the *notaire* who was selling the property. This was refused, so I made a second offer before the end of February. It took much longer for a reply to the second offer to emerge. I later learned that this was because the house had been owned by a lady who had died in her nineties, and the beneficiaries of her will were widely scattered around the globe.

With my offer accepted, the *notaire* (the same *notaire* who was handling the sale) got to work on the conveyance but, because of various delays such as property searches, it was not until May that all was ready.

So it was that on 22 May 1989 we went to the *notaire*'s office and went through the *acte de vente* with him and with one of the vendors. When all was done, we left with the keys and celebrated our purchase. One of the vendors came round later and happily showed us the location of various plots of land that were not immediately obviously ours.

MOVING IN

Before we could move in, the first requirement was to have a drainage and sewage system put in and to rewire the house. Before we could do that we needed to decide how we would use it. It was not until my visit in July that work began on the rewiring, the provision of the bathroom and the sewage and drainage system. By my return in September this had still not been completed.

This highlights the problem of controlling the progress of work while absent. It is, I fear, the tendency of builders the world over to respond first to the nearest, most visible, client and leave the furthest away for another day. What does not have to be done today is thus left until tomorrow. When I was there, progress was made in a series of giant leaps forward. When I was away there were troughs of inactivity. The restoration of the roof, work on the inside surfaces of the walls and the laying of cement and tiles downstairs was not completed until Easter 1990 when our furniture arrived. This was brought over by a UK shipper found in the overseas property pages of the Sunday papers.

Perhaps surprisingly, one of the most time-consuming tasks was organizing the equipping of the house with all the small things: light bulbs, tin openers, potato peelers, loo paper, disinfectant, bleach, saucepans and so on. This is a particular bind if you are setting up a holiday home, a second home, as it is not a simple matter of shipping out everything you have in the UK, but of equipping a home from scratch. The costs soon mount up if you have to buy larger household goods, such as microwaves and duvets, unless you take various items out each summer. We seem to have bought a second set of most things, but it does not stop the car, an estate car now, from being so fully loaded on each trip that I may soon have to buy a trailer.

Our summer 'holiday' of 1990 was spent cleaning and decorating. Of that period, it can truly be said that never in the history of decorating has so much paint been applied by so few hands over such a long period. (With apologies to Cicero.)

We also spent a number of days in the sale rooms of La Rochelle competing with the locals for the additional furniture we needed. Viewing was done in the mornings and the auctions took place in the afternoons. This allowed many of those concerned, including us, to have a good lunch in the cafe opposite.

By 1991 some work still remained to be done. If I were to go through the process again, I would most certainly make use of a *maître d'oeuvre* to oversee the work and maintain the tempo of progress. So, allowing for the work which remains to be done, total expenditure is likely to be around £38,500 which is ten percent above budget. However, this not too bad given the behaviour of the exchange rate and the need to restore the roof which was in a worse condition than I first imagined.

BEING THERE

The house is located on the edge of a village in the Charente valley and has a poplar plantation at the foot of the garden through which we walk to the meadows and the village. There is a butcher and baker but no candlestick maker, two small village general stores, a ladies' hairdresser and two cafes. The nearest large town, Saintes, is some eight kilometres away and liberally stocked with the sort of supermarkets that would give Sainsbury's the collywobbles.

We have found people to be friendly and hospitable. Our neighbours, for example, insist we must use their swimming pool whenever we feel like it. While work was underway on the house I stayed with a peasant farmer in the next village. There, evening meals across an enormous table gave a wonderful insight into the state of local political conflict which, it seemed to me, owed more to family rivalries than to politics. Indeed, I concluded that cousins in France, or at least Charente, occupy a role akin to that of brothers in the Old Testament. Somehow it all reminded me of Suffolk 30 years ago.

The mayor of the *commune* has a sense of humour and we first came across this in the *commune* newsletter where an item reported that the council had decided the shutters of all the houses on a certain route (including ours) were to be painted a specified colour. As this would have meant repainting our shutters I was not best pleased, to put it mildly, and set about raising the banner of civil insurrection. Mercifully this had not quite reached the point of no return when I noticed the date of the newsletter. It was April Fools' Day.

Being there, or rather, not being here, also provides a different perspective on UK politics. Phrases like 'Britain now holds its head high in the Councils of Europe' sound curiously old-fashioned on the French side of the water. It seems outmoded and anachronistic, and out of phase with attitudes there today. Indeed, in Charente Maritime the attitude to politicians is one of cynical amusement and they are not held in high esteem. Nor are Parisians. Both are regarded with suspicion and decent folk do not go to Royan, our nearest resort, in August, when they are there.

Staying in France meant that the whole of Europe seemed to

be accessible without effort. We could go where we wanted when we wanted with no more planning than remembering to lock the house before getting into the car. The feeling of freedom one experiences when able to travel without the time constraints and deadlines imposed by ferry bookings was a revelation. Undoubtedly this was one of the better unexpected advantages of buying a house in France. What a pity the English will not be able to drive through the Channel Tunnel.

TRAVEL ROUTE

As time has passed I have increasingly come to realize the importance of getting settled into a good route as ease of access is going to have an important bearing on the enjoyment your house will give you.

I do not intend to add to the points made earlier about access routes and Channel crossings but to concentrate on my experience of the carriers themselves. Frankly, there is not a lot to choose between them and it is really a matter of finding a carrier with minimum drawbacks from your own point of view. If food is important to you, then the best is on Brittany Ferries and they keep the restaurant open for longer than most. By contrast the others allow you to eat only when they want you to eat.

From experience, I would advise against travelling overnight by ferry. As well as being noisy, ferry operators have been known to re-allocate cabins should the boat used for the crossing have fewer than originally planned. What annoyed me, on the occasion it happened to me, was that I was a member of the property owners' club. But, despite this, they bounced me out of my cabin reservation on the basis that earliest bookings came first. Naturally enough, as a regular traveller, I had booked weeks rather than months earlier, and so did not get a cabin. So they were offering a worse service to their most regular passengers, who they clearly viewed as a captive market. In one sense I am grateful, as it left me in no doubt that the club had little to do with offering the passenger an improved service, but everything to do with boosting their profits.

On my outward journeys, I travel on Saturday afternoon

sailings and stay overnight in an hotel. At about £10 it is cheap compared with the £25 charged for a cabin and one also has a better night's sleep as ferries throb and vibrate and hotels do not. I can leave the hotel very early in the morning, before the night boat has arrived and unloaded. This start and the deserted Sunday morning roads allow me to be at my house by lunchtime. So, although the 24-hour travelling time may seem a lot, in fact it is rather stress-free.

The inward journey is not so smooth and on my last return crossing I tried to break out of the Ouistreham/Portsmouth route by using Seacat and travelling from Cherbourg to Portsmouth. Sadly, everything went wrong. The Seacat failed to arrive and so we took an alternative boat to Weymouth. It was spartan, to say the least, and, after a five-hour crossing, it ran aground on a bright sunny day with good visibility, though the captain still managed to blame adverse weather conditons. A further two hours were required to get the boat off the mud and us off the boat. Then I contrived to get lost. After a disaster of that magnitude it is not going to be easy to persuade my family to experiment with anything. Of course delays can be caused by genuinely bad weather. My first experience of this occurred in February 1990 when gales stopped sailings from Ouistreham. Ferries were, however, still running from Calais, which is five to six hours' drive away. But what do you do if it is six in the evening when you learn of the problem and you have already been driving for seven hours? You wait. How long will you have to wait? You do not know because nobody will tell you when the boat you are waiting for will be able to leave Portsmouth.

Thirty-six hours in Ouistreham in February in a storm. The only redeeming feature was the presence of many other English house-seekers waiting for the boat that never was. We exchanged stories of our experiences. One man told of how he arrived at the Ouistreham *douane* from England in a UK-registered Peugeot 504 estate with a large window frame on the roof rack. A customs man waved him down, peered through the car side window and saw a further four window frames. The customs man demanded the papers but the driver alas had none. The *douanier* asked again, waving a large stamp, but he still had none. The Englishman looked suitably solemn and contrite at his lapse. The customs man raised his eyes to heaven at this typical piece of *Rosbif* stupidity and then, as there were no papers to stamp, waved him through.

Looking back over some ten return journeys over the last two years I suppose one in four or five have suffered some form of disruption which dislocated the timetable. The problem is, of course, that one is unable to predict when it will happen.

Of course one need not be limited to sea and road. One can always fly. Indeed one can, and our two daughters did just that this summer. They flew to Bordeaux, our nearest airport, and we drove to meet them. Thus we learned the truth of the local proverb 'allow one hour to get to Bordeaux and one hour to get from Bordeaux to the airport'. There, they have a nice little earner at the airport of which Arthur Daley would be proud. As in most airports, one pays to park by the hour. However, if you try to pay in advance to avoid the inevitable rush which occurs when passengers clear customs, you find that if you do not get to the exit within 15 minutes you have to pay again, even if you have not exceeded the hours for which you have already paid. The tariff is at eye level in English, but the notice about the nice little earner is at hand level, is well below and only in French. You have been warned. You cannot win. You have to queue.

I wonder what delights the Channel Tunnel will bring?

SUMMARY

- Finding it
- Buying it
- Moving in
- Being there
- Travel route

APPENDICES

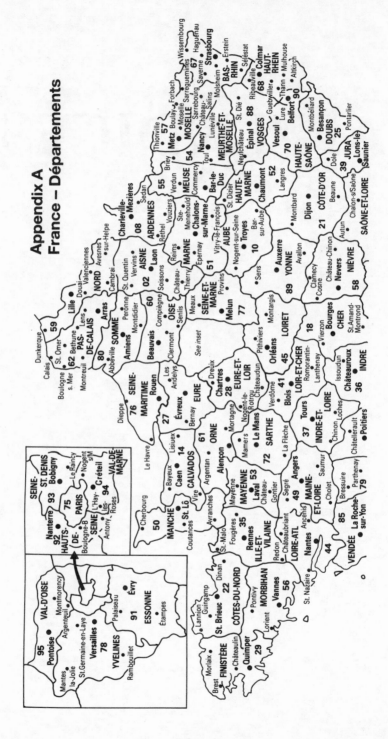

Appendix A
France – Départements

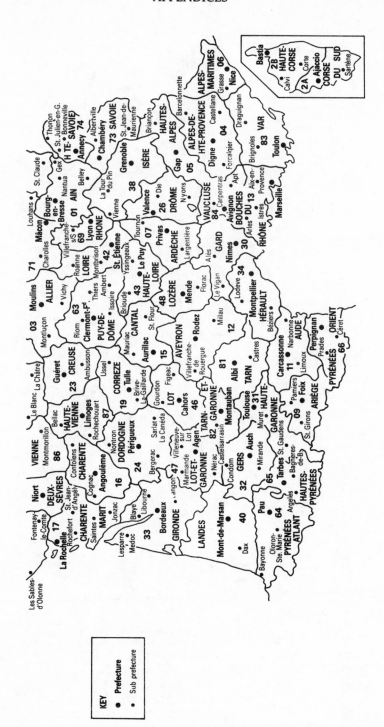

Appendix B
Main routes and motorways

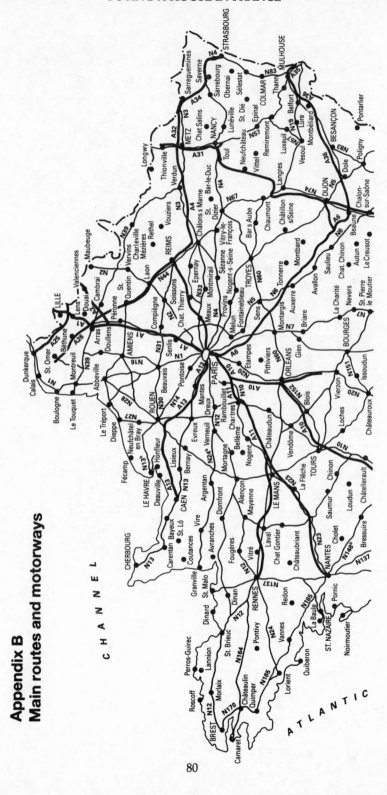

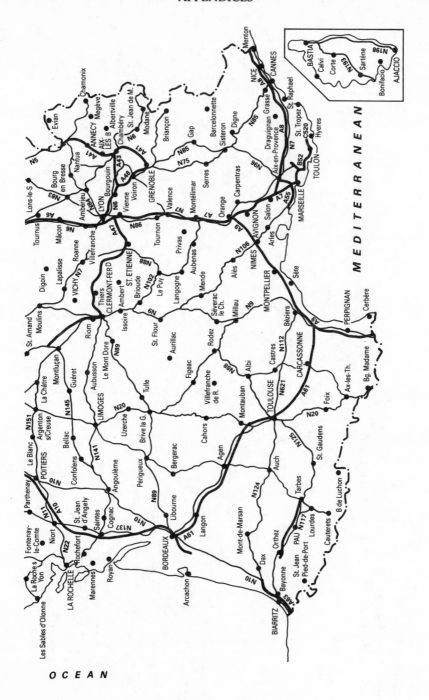

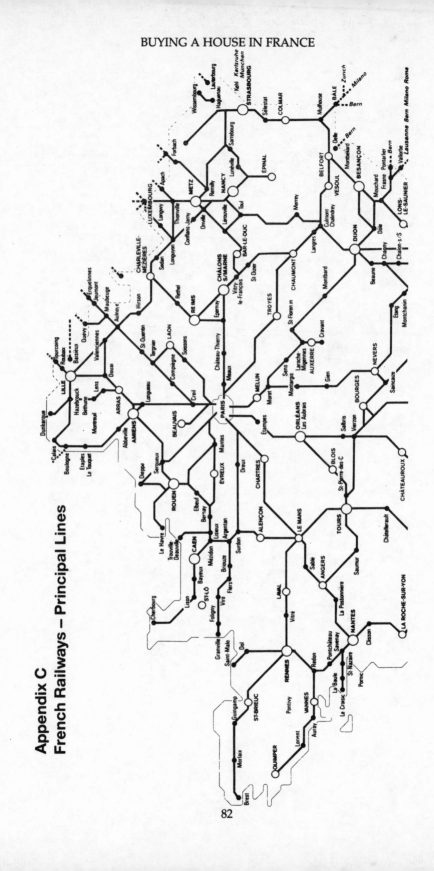

Appendix C
French Railways – Principal Lines

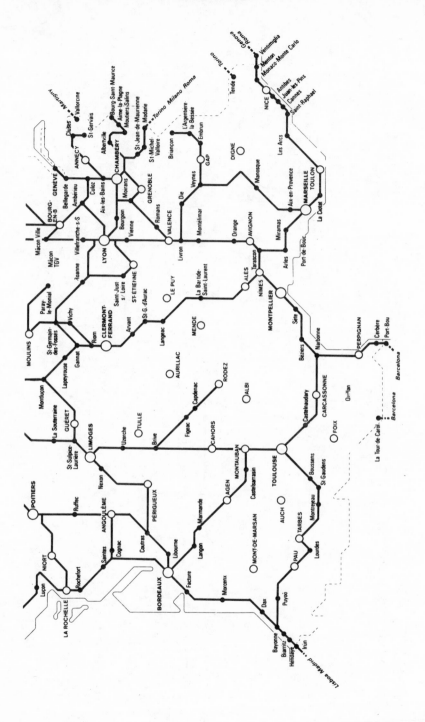

**Appendix D
TGV Routes**

CALAIS
LILLE
ROUEN
PARIS
BREST
RENNES
QUIMPER
LE MANS
ORLÉANS
ANGERS
NANTES
DIJON
BESANÇON
BERNE
LE CREUSOT
CHALON
LAUSANNE
POITIERS
MÂCON
GENEVE
LA ROCHELLE
ANNECY
ANGOULÊME
LYON
CHAMBERY
BORDEAUX
GRENOBLE
AVIGNON
NICE
BIARRITZ
MONTPELLIER
MARSEILLE
TOULOUSE

——— Now
– – – 1992
·········· 1993

Appendix E
Useful Addresses

French Government Tourist Office
178 Piccadilly
London W1
071 491–7622

French Consulate General
21 Cromwell Road
London SW7 2EN
071 581–5292
(Southern England)

French Consulate General
11 Randolph Crescent
Edinburgh EH3 7TT
031 225–7954/5
(Scotland)

French Consulate General
525/535 Cunard Building
Liverpool L3 1ET
051 236–1156
(Northern England and
Northern Ireland)

French Railways Ltd
179 Piccadilly
London W1
071 409–3518 (Motorail)
071 409–1224 (Enquiries)

P&O European Ferries
Channel House
Channel View Road
Dover CT17 9TJ
0304–203388

Brittany Ferries
Millbay Docks
Plymouth PL1 3DU
0752–227941

Sealink UK Ltd
Charter House
Park Street
Ashford
Kent TN24 8EX
0233–647047

Air France
158 New Bond Street
London W1
071 499–9511

Appendix F

French/English Letter to *Office de Tourisme*

Monsieur,
Désireux d'acheter une propriété dans le département du
I hope to buy a property in the département *of*

je vous écris pour demander les adresses des
and I am writing to ask you for some addresses

Syndicats d'Initiative ainsi qu'une documentation
of Syndicats d'Initiative *and some information that will allow*

me permettant de mieux connaître le département. (Journaux,
me to get to know the département *a little better. (Newspapers*

dépliants, etc.)
brochures, etc.)

En vous remerciant à l'avance de votre aide, veuillez agréer,
Thanking you in advance for your help, I remain,

Monsieur, l'expression de mes sentiments distingués.
Yours sincerely,

Appendix G

French/English Letter to *Syndicat d'Initiative*

Monsieur,
Désireux d'acheter une propriété dans la région, je
I hope to buy a property in the area, and I am writing

vous écris pour demander quelques adresses de
to ask for some addresses of

notaires et d'agents immobiliers dans la région ainsi qu'une
notaires *and estate agents in the area and some information*

documentation me permettant de connaître un peu
that will allow me to get to know the département *a little*

le département.
better.

En vous remerciant à l'avance de votre aide, veuillez
Thanking you in advance for your help, I remain,

agréer, Monsieur, l'expression de mes sentiments distingués.
Yours sincerely,

Appendix H

French/English Letter to *Agents Immobiliers/Notaires*

Monsieur, (*use* maître *for a* notaire)
Désireux d'acheter une propriété dans la région, je
I hope to buy a property in the area and I am writing

vous écris pour indiquer le genre de maison que je
to you to describe the sort of house I am looking for, in the

recherche, dans l'espoir que vous puissiez me faire parvenir
hope that you will be able to send me

les descriptions de quelques propriétés que vous avez à
the details of some of the properties that you have for

vendre.
sale.

Je vous contacterai ultérieurement pour prendre rendez-vous
I will contact you at a later date for visiting

pour visiter des propriétés qui auront retenu mon attention.
those properties that I have found of interest.

Je recherche une maison de campagne/de ville/ de village
I am looking for a house in the country/town house/village house

/ancienne/neuve à rénover/sans travaux importants/
/old house/ new house to renovate/without major work/

habitable de suite/ avec sanitaires et avec un petit jardin/
ready to live in/ with bathroom, WC and with a small garden/

avec un grand jardin/ avec beaucoup de terrain.
with a large garden/ with a lot of land.

Je recherche (nombre) pièces et mon prix de départ sera de
I am looking for (number) rooms and my starting price is

. . . .Frs tous frais compris.
. . . .francs including all tax.

En vous remerciant à l'avance, croyez Monsieur/Maître, a
Thanking you in advance estate agent/notaire,

l'expression de mes sentiments distingués.
Yours sincerely,

(Please note that the number of rooms quoted must include all
the rooms and not just the bedrooms.)

Appendix I
Useful Terms

OUTSIDE

surroundings   *les environs*(m)
shop   *le commerce*
doctor   *le docteur*
lake   *le lac*
fishing   *la pêche*
seaside resort   *la station balnéaire*
golf course   *le terrain de golf*
flower garden   *le jardin d'agrément*
landscaped garden   *le jardin payage*
walled garden   *le jardin clos de murs*
enclosed garden   *le jardin clos*
wide views   *la vue panoramique*
main house   *l'habitation principale* (f)
outbuilding   *la dépendance*
main drains   *le tout à l'égout*
closed septic tank (i.e., needs emptying)   *la fosse étanche*
septic tank (i.e., that self-drains)   *la fosse septique*
wire fence   *la clôture en fil de fer*
land   *le terrain*
paddock   *l'enclos*(m)
drinking water   *l'eau potable*(f)
school   *l'école*(f)
chemist   *la pharmacie*
swimming pool   *la piscine*
river   *la rivière*
hunting   *la chasse*
riding   *l'équitation* (f)
tennis   *le tennis*
garage   *le garage*
vegetable garden   *le potager*
shed   *le chai*
stable   *l'écurie*(f)
country   *la campagne*
well   *le puits*

THE HOUSE

central heating   *le chauffage central*
oil-fired central heating   *le chauffage central au fuel mazout*
hall   *l'entrée*(f)
landing   *le palier* ⎱ All of these may be replaced by   *le dégagement*
corridor   *le couloir* ⎰   if they are on the small side
bathroom   *la salle de bain*
living-room   *la salle de séjour*
dining-room   *la salle à manger*
shower-room   *la salle d'eau*
bedroom   *la chambre*
kitchen   *la cuisine*
basement   *le sous-sol*
vault   *la cave voutée*
loft   *le grenier*
cellar   *la cave*
WC   *le cabinet de toilette*
workshop   *l'atelier*(m)
loft which is convertible   *le grenier aménageable*
shower   *la douche*
room   *la pièce*
room with high ceiling   *la pièce haute de plafond*
room with a low ceiling   *la pièce basse de plafond*
floor   *l'étage*(m)
ground floor   *le rez-de-chaussée*
first floor   *le premier étage*
second floor   *le deuxième étage*
exposed beam   *la poutre apparente*
window-ledge   *le rebord de fenêtre*
chimney   *la cheminée*
staircase   *l'escalier*(m)
other room   *l'autre pièce*(f)
window   *la fenêtre*
door   *la porte*
window-pane   *la vitre*
bulb   *l'ampoule*(f)
light-fitting   *la douille*

MATERIALS

tile   *la tuile*
wall   *le mur*
brick   *la brique*
insulation   *l'isolant*(m)
fibreglass   *la laine de verre*
carpet   *la moquette*
joist   *la solive*
gutter   *la gouttière*
slate   *l'ardoise*(f)
stone   *la pierre*
breeze-block   *le parpaing*
tiled floor   *le carrelage*
wooden floor   *le parquet*
paint   *la peinture*
plumbing   *la plomberie*
pipe   *la conduite*

DIMENSIONS

For the house this is usually given in square metres, e.g., *150 m² habitable* = 150 square metres (1,614 sq ft) living area in all, and this may all be on one floor, *au sol* (ground coverage). If not, you may find added *sur x étages* = on *x* floors, where *x* is the number of floors.

For the land, the dimensions may be given in square metres (m²) or in   *ares* and   *centiares*, e.g.:
10 ares 40 centiares = 1,040 m² (11,193 sq ft)
9 ares 30 centiares = 930 m² (10,010 sq ft)
100 ares = 10,000 m² = 1 hectare (2.47 acres)
(Note: 1 acre = approx. 4,027 m²)

Appendix J

French/English Letter asking to receive newspaper

Monsieur,

Résident en Angleterre et desireux d'acheter une maison
Living in England and wishing to buy a house

en France, je voudrais recevoir chez moi en Angleterre votre
in France I would like to receive at home in England your

publication.
paper.

Veuillez avoir l'obligeance de me faire parvenir
Therefore I would ask you to send me your

vos tarifs d'abonnement.
subscription costs.

En vous remerciant à l'avance de votre aide, veuillez agréer,
Thanking you in advance for your help, I remain,

Monsieur, l'expression de mes sentiments distingués.
Yours sincerely,

Appendix K

French/English Letter asking for services connection

Monsieur,

Ayant acheté une maison située à (give full address)
Having bought a house situated at (full address),

anciennement la propriété de M. (give name) je voudrais
previously the property of Mr (give name) I would like an

prendre rendez-vous avec vos services pour l'alimentation
appointment with your service for connection

en eau/gaz/ électricité le branchement du téléphone.
with water/gas/electricity/telephone.

En vous remerciant à l'avance de votre aide, veuillez agréer,
Thanking you in advance for your help, I remain,

Monsieur, l'expression mes sentiments distingués.
Yours sincerely,

Appendix L
Motorail Services

FROM	TO
Boulogne	Avignon
	Biarritz
	Bordeaux
	Brive
	Fréjus/St Raphael
	Nantes
	Narbonne
	Toulouse
Calais	Moutiers
	Narbonne
	Nice
Dieppe	Avignon
	Fréjus/St Raphael

With the exception of Calais/Nice and Calais/Moutiers, the services are available from approximately mid-May to mid-October.

INDEX